SCIENCE EXPLORER

FORECASTING A FLOOD

Follow the Clues

by Tamra B. Orr

CHERRY LAKE PUBLISHING · ANN ARBOR, MICHIGAN

Published in the United States of America by Cherry Lake Publishing
Ann Arbor, Michigan
www.cherrylakepublishing.com

CONTENT EDITOR: Robert Wolffe, EdD, Professor of Teacher Education, Bradley University, Peoria, Illinois
BOOK DESIGN AND ILLUSTRATION: The Design Lab
READING ADVISER: Marla Conn, ReadAbility, Inc.

PHOTO CREDITS: Cover and page 1, ©Dan Schreiber/Shutterstock, Inc.; pages 4 and 19, ©Tyler Olson/ Shutterstock, Inc.; page 5, ©Jerry Sharp/Shutterstock, Inc.; page 6, ©withGod/Shutterstock, Inc.; page 7, ©Owen Fitzpatrick/Shutterstock, Inc.; page 8, ©Ryan McGinnis/Alamy; page 9, ©Zocchi Roberto/ Shutterstock, Inc.; page 10, ©Marafona/Shutterstock, Inc.; page 11, ©Bas Meelker/Shutterstock, Inc.; page 12, ©bikeriderlondon/Shutterstock, Inc.; page 13, ©Christian Mueller/Shutterstock, Inc.; page 15, ©Jeff Greenberg/Alamy; page 16, ©cristovao/Shutterstock, Inc.; page 17, ©ChameleonsEye/Shutterstock, Inc.; page 18, ©Budimir Jevtic/Shutterstock, Inc.; page 20, ©David R. Frazier Photolibrary, Inc./Alamy; page 22, ©Vladimir Yudin/Dreamstime.com; page 23, ©taro911 Photographer/Shutterstock, Inc.; page 24, ©Whytock/Shutterstock, Inc.; page 26, ©Thor Jorgen Udvang/Shutterstock, Inc.; page 27, ©ejwhite/ Shutterstock, Inc.; page 28, ©Ricardo Reitmeyer/Shutterstock, Inc.; page 29, ©Pixsooz/Shutterstock, Inc.

LIBRARY OF CONGRESS CATALOGING-IN-PUBLICATION DATA
Orr, Tamra, author.
 Forecasting a flood / by Tamra B. Orr.
 pages cm. — (Science explorer. Follow the clues)
 Audience: Grades 4 to 6.
 Summary: "Use the scientific method to learn how experts predict floods and other
natural disasters."—Provided by publisher.
 Includes bibliographical references and index.
 ISBN 978-1-62431-778-1 (lib. bdg.) — ISBN 978-1-62431-788-0 (pbk.) — ISBN 978-1-
62431-808-5 (ebook) —ISBN 978-1-62431-798-9 (pdf)
 1. Flood forecasting—Juvenile literature. 2. Floods—Juvenile literature. 3. Floods—Safety
measures—Juvenile literature. 4. Weather forecasting—Juvenile literature. I. Title.

 GB1399.2.O77 2014
 551.48'9—dc23   2013042106

Cherry Lake Publishing would like to acknowledge the work of The Partnership for 21st Century Skills.
Please visit www.p21.org for more information.

Printed in the United States of America, Corporate Graphics Inc.
January 2014

TABLE OF CONTENTS

CHAPTER 1

PREDICTING THE WEATHER

Julian could not wait for his mom to visit his class.

Julian looked up and smiled. It was 8:30 a.m. He had been watching the clock since he had arrived at school. Today his mom was coming to his class to talk about weather. Mrs. Higgins was a **meteorologist**. Besides doing daily weather reports on television, she helped people learn about natural disasters. It had been raining heavily off and on for the past week where Julian lived. The wide Red River that ran near the town had been rising steadily. As the river came closer to flooding, Julian's teacher, Mr. Yang, had asked Mrs. Higgins to visit the class.

"We have a special guest today," said Mr. Yang, Julian's teacher. "Many of you will recognize her from the nightly news. This is Janice Higgins. She is here to talk to us about floods."

"Hello, everyone," said Mrs. Higgins, as she walked to the front of the room. "I am so glad to be here today. Floods are amazing! They remind us how powerful water can be. People like me, along with other experts, spend a lot of time studying floods. By looking at weather reports, we can help predict when floods are going to happen and warn people so they stay safe."

Lucia raised her hand. "My dad says that the weather report is usually wrong as often as it is right. Is that true?"

"That is a great question," said Mrs. Higgins. "Predicting the weather can be difficult, even with the high-tech equipment we use. Let me explain why. Think how long it takes you to get ready for school every

Floods can be extremely dangerous, especially when they occur without any warning.

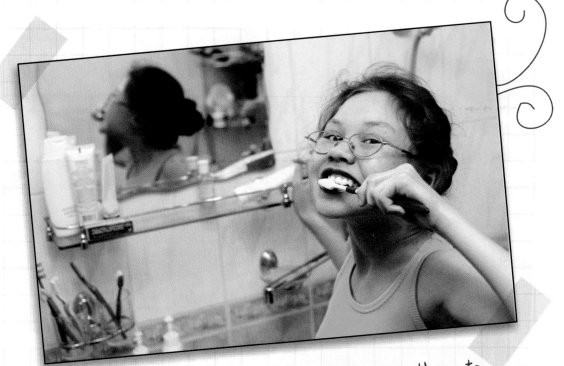

People can predict how long it will take them to get ready in the morning based on past experience.

morning. Let's say it takes you one hour from the time you wake up to when you get on the school bus.

"From past experience, you know it takes you about an hour to wake up, take a shower, get dressed, eat breakfast, grab your backpack, and make it to the bus stop on time. You can predict that tomorrow it will take you an hour to do it all again. That is what all the signs are telling you."

Many students nodded.

"But suppose someone in your family is already in the bathroom when you go for your shower. What if you get dressed and you spill orange juice on your pants and have to change clothes? Or what if you can't find your homework assignment, so you don't leave your house when you planned? These factors can change how long it will take you to get to the bus stop. Suddenly, it might take you 90 minutes—and you'll likely miss the bus."

"Predictions are not always right, then," said Mr. Yang.

"Exactly," said Mrs. Higgins. "Despite everything you knew and planned, there are factors that can change your prediction. In the world of weather, we consider factors such as wind direction, air pressure, and the development of storms. But sometimes they don't behave as we expect them to. Wind direction can change, air pressure can rise or drop, or storm fronts can develop very quickly. When factors don't happen as expected, we need to change and update our weather predictions.

"Tell your dad that as we learn more, our predictions will become more and more accurate," Mrs. Higgins added, smiling.

Winds may change direction or speed unexpectedly, and change the weather.

"Storm chasers" study weather in the field

The three types of people most involved in studying weather events such as flooding are geologists, hydrologists, and meteorologists.

☆ Geologists study Earth's surface and its interior, such as rocks, minerals, metals, and water. They work to understand the history of our planet to help them predict future events like floods, earthquakes, and eruptions of volcanoes.

☆ Meteorologists study weather, climate, and other elements of the **atmosphere**. They usually work in weather stations and laboratories, as well as in the field.

☆ Hydrologists study the waters of our planet. They study water that is on and below the earth's surface and in the atmosphere. They also work to improve the quality of the water and to find new sources of water on Earth. Hydrologists work in labs and out in the field, and must have a strong background in the natural sciences.

8

CHAPTER 2

THE REASONS FOR FLOODS

What makes a body of water, such as a lake, flood?

"Did you know that floods are one of the most common natural disasters in North America?" asked Mrs. Higgins. "There are more than 5,000 floods every year in the United States. That is more than any other country in the world.

"Who can define what a flood is?" asked Mrs. Higgins.

Tyson raised his hand and called out, "A bunch of water!"

"Yes, but not just water. Rivers, lakes, and oceans are a bunch of water," she said. "What else turns water into a flood?"

"Water in the wrong place?" asked Marcia.

↖ Hurricanes can cause giant waves and storm surges.

"Exactly! A flood happens when an area has too much water. The excess water ends up going into areas where it is not usually found, or where it should not be," said Mrs. Higgins. "First, we need to find out what causes too much water to be in a place."

Mrs. Higgins picked up a marker and walked to the whiteboard.

"We have to gather information and study it. So far, we have found that floods occur for four main reasons."

On the board she wrote,

- heavy rain due to storms
- storm **surges** on the ocean
- snow melting too quickly
- dams or **levees** breaking

Pointing to the first reason, Mrs. Higgins said, "There are more than 10,000 severe storms each year in the United States. Many bring very heavy rain. There can be a lot of rain at once, as we've had in this town, or rainfall over a long period of time."

Referring to the second and third reasons on the list, she said, "Hurricanes and tropical storms cause oceans to rise and send huge waves onto shore. And when winter snows melt too early or too fast, it can also result in a flood.

"The fourth reason for flooding is a combination of the weather and man-made constructions," Mrs. Higgins continued. "If a dam or levee is not strong enough or is damaged, it can break trying to hold back more

↖ Some levees are made up of large mounds of soil.

water than usual. For example, if a dam made of soil gets too wet, the dam can weaken and collapse."

Kendra raised her hand. "Why doesn't all of the extra rain soak into the ground, like when I water our garden at home?"

"That is another factor we consider when we make flood predictions based on weather predictions. We gather information about the ground. Normally, **precipitation** falls to the earth and is soaked up, or absorbed, by the ground. Then it goes into underground rivers. If the ground is frozen, however, it cannot soak up the rain. Also, once soil is completely soaked, the water starts to build up. Can anyone think of another reason some ground can't absorb the water?"

Sometimes, it rains so hard that the ground cannot absorb all the water.

Water usually flows into drains along streets or sidewalks in cities.

Julian raised his hand. "Concrete and asphalt can't absorb water," he explained. "That means floods are especially dangerous in cities, where most ground is made of those."

Mrs. Higgins grinned and replied, "And so a lot of the rain just runs off into drains and ends up in streams and rivers, which can overflow and cause flooding.

"Now that we've talked about why floods happen, let's look at the possibility of floods in our town," said Mrs. Higgins.

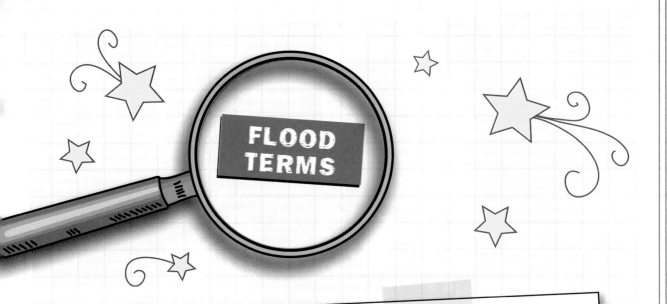

FLOOD TERMS

Have you ever wondered about the difference between a weather watch and a weather warning? The difference is based on how likely the event is to happen. You've probably heard watches and warnings for snowstorms, tornadoes, and hurricanes on the television and radio, or seen them on the Internet. If the chance of a flood is likely, weather centers issue a watch. This tells people to pay close attention to weather reports and take precautions in case a flood starts. If the flood is about to happen or has already begun, a warning is issued. Warnings mean take cover and get to safety immediately.

Typically, weather centers issue regular flood watches and warnings when unusual amounts of water may flow or are already flowing onto land that is usually dry. The effects of these floods can last for days or even weeks. Flash flood watches are usually issued within minutes or an hour after intense rains. The watch becomes a warning when flash floods are actually occurring. Coastal flood watches, as their name implies, are issued along coastlines if seawater rises unexpectedly.

CHAPTER 3

COLLECTING INFORMATION

The scientific method can help answer questions about anything from weather prediction to crop growth.

"We've learned what floods are, and what usually causes them," Mr. Yang reminded the class. "What happens next, Mrs. Higgins?"

"Let's look at how likely a flood might be here. To do this, we can use the scientific method. This is a process that scientists use to find the answer to a question. The process doesn't always work the same way. But usually the scientific method works like this." Julian's mom wrote on the whiteboard:

Predicting the weather is more than just guesswork.

THE SCIENTIFIC METHOD
1. Ask a question
2. Gather information and observe/research
3. Make a **hypothesis**—or guess the answer
4. Experiment to test your hypothesis
5. **Analyze** your test results
6. Present a conclusion

When Mrs. Higgins had finished, Marcia raised her hand. "How will the scientific method help us predict flooding?"

"Let's start with the first item on the list," Mrs. Higgins replied. What is a question we can ask?"

"Will it flood today?" Michael guessed.

"That's a great question," said Mrs. Higgins. "Next we make observations. We know that it's been raining heavily in this area, and that the river level has been rising. We need to gather a little more information on exactly how much it is raining and how quickly the river is rising before we make a hypothesis."

"We can use rain **gauges** to measure how much it is raining," said Marcia. "We have one outside our school."

"Exactly," said Mrs. Higgins. "That's one of the rain gauges I use to track the weather in this area. We should also keep track of how quickly the river is rising. We can visit the Red River Weather Web site online.

↖ Rain gauges help measure how much rain falls in an area.

The site has a live video of the river's depth gauge that you can watch. We'll use that to see how deep the river is." Julian's mom looked down at her watch. "It's 9:00 a.m. now. Let's check the rain gauge outside and river gauge now, and again in an hour. Then we'll form a hypothesis."

Mrs. Higgins drew a table on the whiteboard next to the steps of the scientific method.

Time	Rainfall	River Depth

Many rivers have permanent gauges to measure their depth.

You can find up-to-date information about river depth and other weather facts online.

At 9:00 a.m. and 10:00 a.m., the students checked the data and wrote it down on the whiteboard. Then Mrs. Higgins announced, "Now it's time we take a look at the numbers." She pointed to the whiteboard. "The river was 37 feet 11.5 inches deep at 9:00 a.m. By 10:00 a.m., the river was 38 feet deep. In that time it rained about one half inch. With this information, we can create a hypothesis. Does anyone remember our scientific question?"

Julian raised his hand. "The question was: Will the Red River flood today?"

To form a hypothesis about the weather, meteorologists gather information from equipment both in space and on the ground.

"Correct," Mrs. Higgins said with a proud smile. "The Red River is at flood stage when it is 40 feet deep. Okay, class, what do you think? Will it reach 40 feet today?" Nearly all the students raised their hands to try and answer.

"Let's take a vote," said Mr. Yang. "Raise your hand if you think it will flood today." He stopped and counted. "Now who thinks it will not flood?" He counted the hands again. "The majority of students voted that it is going to flood."

Mrs. Higgins nodded. "That will be our hypothesis. Next, we experiment and analyze our results. Let's check the river depth and rain gauge for the next few hours, and then we'll see what we find out!"

MAJOR FLOODS

There have been a number of destructive floods throughout history. One of the earliest was in Johnstown, Pennsylvania, in the spring of 1889. Huge amounts of rain caused a local dam to break. Twenty million gallons (76 million liters) of water gushed into the city, completely wiping it out. A few years later, a Category 4 hurricane struck the island of Galveston, Texas. After a storm surge hit, a U.S. Weather Service reporter stated, "In reality, there was no island, just the ocean with houses standing out of the waves which rolled between them." In 1993, the Mississippi River stayed at flood stage for almost three months, so that event became known as "the flood that came and stayed forever."

The most recent floods to strike the United States were in 2005 and 2013. Hurricane Katrina struck the Gulf Coast in the late summer of 2005. Eighty percent of New Orleans was flooded when levees broke. It took weeks for the water to **recede**. It was considered one of the worst natural disasters in the country's history. A flood in Colorado in the late summer of 2013 destroyed or damaged thousands of homes and dozens of bridges due to huge and unexpected amounts of rain.

CHAPTER 4

PUTTING THE DETAILS TOGETHER

↳ A line graph like the one used by Julian's class can keep track of changes over time.

As the day progressed, the students turned their data into a line graph. The chart showed how quickly the river depth increased compared to how much it rained. Each time they checked the river and rain gauges, they added dots to the graph.

By the end of the day, everyone was excited to see the results of their weather study. The whiteboard was now full of the data they had collected. Just before the last hour of the school day, Mrs. Higgins walked back to the front of the classroom.

"Last time we measured the depth of the Red River, it was just below 39 feet," said Mrs. Higgins, pointing to the number on the whiteboard. "What do you think of our original hypothesis? Will it still flood today?"

As it continued to rain, Julian's classmates revisited whether or not the Red River would flood.

Marcia quickly raised her hand. "Can I change my vote?" she asked.

"Of course you can," said Mr. Yang. Changing your forecast based on new data is part of being a good scientist. Now let's check the river and the rain gauge one more time and find out for certain if the river flooded."

"It's a flood!" Lucia announced from the classroom's computer. "I can see in the video that the river is just above 40 feet."

Mr. Yang wrote the information on the table and added it to the line chart. "We have our conclusion, then," he said when he finished. "It did flood today!"

Meteorologists can describe a river as having different levels of flooding, from minor flooding to major.

TOP 10 FLOOD FAST FACTS

1. Anywhere it can rain, it can flood. This means everyone lives in a flood zone.
2. A car can be carried away by as little as 2 feet (0.6 meters) of water. Six inches (15 centimeters) of fast-moving water is enough to knock down an adult human.
3. Ninety percent of all the national events classified by the president as natural disasters involve some type of flooding.
4. A few inches of water can cause thousands of dollars in damage to homes.
5. In 2011, flood damages totaled $8.41 billion and resulted in 113 deaths in the United States.
6. Floods kill more people, on average, than lightning, tornadoes, or hurricanes.
7. Nearly half of all deaths due to floods occur in automobiles as they are pushed downstream by rushing water.
8. Along the East Coast, as well as the Gulf Coast, the main causes of floods are hurricanes and storms. In the western part of the nation they are due mainly to melting snow and rainstorms.
9. Flooding is the only natural disaster for which the federal government provides insurance.
10. Flash floods have been known to create walls of water 10 to 20 feet (3 m to 6 m) high.

CHAPTER 5

STUDYING A WEATHER WARNING

↳ Sometimes a weather team reports on an event from out in the field.

Tyson looked worried as he raised his hand. "Are we in danger?" he asked.

"The school is far enough from the river that we are not in any danger," said Mrs. Higgins. "Plus, the river has to be much deeper to go above the levee. We are safe. But you bring up a very good question.

"Weather warnings might be quite frightening for some people," she continued, "while other people might not pay any attention to them. Both reactions are a mistake. There are weather warnings for many different types of weather, including flood, severe thunderstorms, tornadoes,

hurricanes, and high winds. The warnings are designed to protect people. We word them very carefully and give as much information as we can so people know what to do.

"Let's take a look at a weather warning and see what we can learn," said Mrs. Higgins as she handed out a sheet of paper to each student. A typical flood warning was printed on the paper.

"Your first clue that there is a weather warning is a loud, annoying sound that comes over your television or radio. The loud sound is designed to get your attention. The first words spoken by the newscaster will probably be, 'The National Weather Service has issued a flash flood warning until . . .'" Then he or she will tell you when the danger or risk will be over. Pay attention to that as it may change in later warnings.

If a weather announcement appears on your television, be sure to listen to what it says.

"Next," said Mrs. Higgins, "the announcement will list the states affected by the warning. That will be followed by the specific counties that are affected, so always listen for the name of your county."

Pointing to words farther down the page, Mrs. Higgins continued, "There will be a short description of why there is a risk of the flood. For example, the warning might say, 'Recent heavy rainfall has caused river levels to rise. Major flooding is forecast.' Then, the warning will end with a reminder to listen for further updates and to take safety precautions," she said.

"Thank you for all of the helpful information, Mrs. Higgins," said Mr. Yang. The class applauded. Julian applauded the loudest. It had been so great to have his mom in class today!

It is a good idea to work out a plan with your family for every emergency.

BEING PREPARED

Hope for the best but prepare for the worst. Make sure you have an emergency plan at home for each type of possible disaster, such as a flood, tornado, or earthquake. In a flood situation, it is a good idea to move valuables and treasured items such as photographs and documents to the highest ground possible. But only if you have time!

You should also stock up on disaster supplies, including:

☆ 1 gallon (3.8 l) of clean water per person per day
☆ battery-powered radio
☆ blankets and pillows
☆ extra clothing, socks, and shoes
☆ first aid kit, including medications
☆ flashlight with batteries
☆ canned food and can opener
☆ food and water for pets
☆ cell phones with chargers
☆ car keys and house keys

GLOSSARY

analyze (AN-uh-lize) to examine something carefully in order to understand it

atmosphere (AT-muhs-feer) the mixture of gases that surrounds a planet; the air in a particular place

gauges (GAYJ-iz) instruments for measuring something

hypothesis (hye-PAH-thi-sis) an idea that could explain how something works but must be proven by the scientific method

levees (LEV-eez) banks built up near rivers to prevent flooding

meteorologist (mee-tee-ur-AHL-uh-jist) a person who studies Earth's atmosphere, especially in relation to weather and climate

precipitation (pri-sip-i-TAY-shuhn) the falling of water from the sky in the form of rain, sleet, hail, or snow

recede (ri-SEED) to move back

surges (SURJ-iz) sudden, strong rushes

FOR MORE INFORMATION

BOOKS

Cameron, Schyrlet. *Scientific Method Investigation: A Step-by-Step Guide for Middle-School Students*. Quincy, IL: Mark Twain Media, 2010.

Koponen, Libby. *Floods*. New York: Scholastic, 2009.

Sepahban, Lois. *Floods*. Minneapolis, Minn.: ABDO Publishing Company, 2013.

Silverstein, Alvin. *Floods: The Science Behind Raging Waters and Mudslides*. Berkeley Heights, N.J.: Enslow Publishers, 2010.

WEB SITES

Biology 4 Kids

www.biology4kids.com/files/studies_scimethod.html

Read more about how the scientific method works.

FEMA—Be a Hero!

www.ready.gov/kids

Play games and learn some tips on how to keep you and your family ready for any disaster.

In Focus: An Online NewsHour Web Site for Students—Floods

www.pbs.org/newshour/infocus/floods.html

Visit this Web site to read stories about flood survivors.

INDEX

ABOUT THE AUTHOR

Tamra B. Orr is an author living in the Pacific Northwest. Orr has a degree in Secondary Education and English from Ball State University. She is the mother to four, and the author of more than 350 books for readers of all ages. When she isn't writing or reading books, she is writing letters to friends all over the world. Although fascinated by all aspects of science, most of her current scientific method skills are put to use tracking down lost socks, missing keys, and overdue library books.